SINGLED OUT

A JOURNEY OF FAITH, RESILIENCE, AND STRATEGIC GUIDANCE

TIANA T. BURNETT

EDITED BY
NICOLE QUEEN

VISION PUBLISHING
HOUSE

To every single mother who feels alone and without hope – you are a wonderful, beautiful being. May you find strength and encouragement within these pages.

CONTENTS

INTRODUCTION

Being a single mom is not an easy journey. It comes with its own set of challenges and uncertainties, requiring immense courage and resourcefulness. I know this because I have walked that path. As a single mom, I faced countless obstacles and had to make difficult choices to ensure a better life for my daughter and me.

The experience of being a single mom has profoundly influenced my perspective on life. It has taught me the true meaning of resilience, faith, and the power of community. Through many trials and tribulations, I have learned to navigate life with the huge responsibility of providing for my child and to redirect my focus from the problem to God. That was the only way I'd be able to provide for my daughter's needs. But being a single mom is not just about navigating the complexities of motherhood. You must also discover the overarching purpose and calling that God has placed upon your life. In those moments when you feel singled out by society or circumstances, it's essential to remember that you are also singled out by God for a unique and meaningful purpose.

INTRODUCTION

As I journeyed through the ups and downs of single motherhood, I realized that being thrust into the role of a mom was not by chance or happenstance. It was a divine calling, a purpose carefully designed by God for me. Amidst sleepless nights, financial struggles, and the weight of a myriad of other responsibilities, I discovered that I was being singled out by God to fulfill His plan.

Being a single mom requires strength and resilience beyond what we can muster on our own. It pushes us to rely on God and seek His divine guidance in our daily lives. Through all the challenges, I found solace in knowing that God had a specific purpose for my life.

In my goal to make ends meet, I became incredibly driven and focused on my career. I pursued education, attending college to secure a better future for my daughter and myself. I vividly remember praying to God, realizing that I would not have the emotional or financial resources I needed. My prayer was simple: "God, don't let us lack in any area of our lives." There were times when even a small amount of money felt like a fortune, and I relied on the support and generosity of others to make it.

God is strategic in all of His interventions with His children, and that includes the people He puts in our lives for a specific reason. One of those moments was with my daughter's "second mom," as she liked to call her. From the first day I took her to church, she immediately fell in love with my daughter. She told me, "She is mine until she turns nine; then you can have her back." She was her babysitter, purchased her school clothes, and Christmas toys until she was nine years old. These were such blessings to me. I did not have to worry about who was going to pick her up from school. Other supportive individuals in my life played a crucial role in our journey, as well.

My God-sister inspired me to obtain my degree, which is why I decided to attend weekend college. After seeing her improve the trajectory of her life by pursuing an advanced degree, I was motivated to obtain my bachelor's degree through the same program. I later pursued and obtained my master's degree, even without taking the GMAT, through a newly established business program at a prestigious college. These educational accomplishments, coupled with promotions in my career, empowered me to provide for my daughter and offer her a better life.

However, my story is not just about personal achievements. It is a testament to the power of faith, prayer, and the strength derived from community support. Throughout my journey, I realized the importance of my church family and the neighborhood community. They became my pillars of strength. The "Baltimore Aunts" helped me watch over my daughter, offering support when I could not afford a babysitter. Yes, I often felt overwhelmed. Although my response to this is a cliché, it captures my true sentiment — but God!

As a single mother, resourcefulness became second nature to me. I learned to navigate life's challenges, finding shortcuts and leveraging every opportunity to provide for my child's well-being. The pressures of being a single parent drive a constant search for survival strategies, demanding a level of resilience that sets us apart. While others may have the luxury of relying on a partner or more resources, single parents have to go the extra mile to ensure their child's future. Single parents have to sustain a balanced future for their children that allows them to be afforded the same opportunities as those in a stable household.

While the world might perceive single moms through a lens of limitations, and some of these limitations may seem valid, God sees inherent strength and boundless potential. He knows the incredible capacity within us to love, nurture, and shape the lives of our children, our inner circle, and our community. He entrusts us with this sacred task, knowing that we are exceptionally equipped for the challenges that lie ahead.

INTRODUCTION

God sees us with an unfiltered lens. He is intimately acquainted with our struggles, every silent fear, every buried dream, and the deepest desires that reside in our hearts. You have been singled out by Him to fulfill a purpose that only you can accomplish. Your experiences, strengths, and even your weaknesses are all integral parts of the tapestry that He weaves together for your contribution to accomplishing His grand design.

However, the concept of being singled out is far-reaching and extends beyond the single mother. It is universal and thus applies to everyone, irrespective of their circumstances. Each of us has a remarkable purpose, a calling that sets us apart and imbues our lives with meaning. Whether you are a single mom, a young professional, or someone on a completely different life path, remember that you are not overlooked or forgotten.

This story is born from my profound desire to share my personal experiences and offer inspiration to those who may be facing similar circumstances. I want to let you know that you are never alone, even in the darkest of times, and that hope persists. Through the highs and lows of my journey, I have witnessed the unmistakable presence of God strategically guiding and supporting me, enabling me to overcome seemingly insurmountable obstacles.

By sharing my story, I aim to encourage and uplift not only single moms but also anyone navigating life's valleys. From the struggles we endure, we can emerge not weakened, but fortified, enriched with wisdom, and with an unshakable faith in the One who consistently provides, sustains, and gently guides us through every trial.

As you delve into the chapters that follow in this book, I invite you to reflect on your own life journey. Consider the profound ways in which you have been singled out by God, regardless of your circumstances. Embrace the bedrock truth that you are chosen, valued, and loved by the Creator.

Drawing from my own experience as a single mom, I hope to inspire and encourage you to embrace your remarkable calling and purpose. I warmly welcome and invite you to join me on this transformative expedition. Together, let's embark on a voyage that explores the immense power of faith, the strength of community, and the resilience within us, all while remembering that each of us is singled out by God to make a difference in the world.

I

THE CONCEPT OF BEING SINGLED OUT

In the intricate, beautiful tapestry of life, each of us is a special thread, deliberately chosen for a distinct purpose. This chapter delves deep into the heart of this profound concept—what it means to be singled out. We will explore the diverse interpretations and perspectives surrounding this notion and discuss the virtuous response to God's divine calling.

SINGLED OUT FOR A PURPOSE

Let me share the profound revelation that has shaped my journey: 'Singled Out.' It represents a double conundrum, reflecting both my role as a single mother and the realization that I've been singled out for a distinctive calling. The truth is, every aspect of my life — every challenge, triumph, joy, and heartache — has been part of divine preparation for something greater.

 "When they had all had enough to eat, he said to his disciples, 'Gather the pieces that are left over. Let nothing be wasted.'"

— JOHN 6:12

There's wisdom in the words of John 6:12 that resonates with me; it teaches us that nothing is wasted. Even when life feels like a relentless series of trials, it's all part of a grand design. I heard someone say, 'It's either working for us or it is working on us.'

Even your tears are not wasted! David, who faced great difficulties in life, prayed while his enemies, the Philistines, had seized him in Gath: 'Record my lament; list my tears on your scroll - are they not in your record?' (Psalm 56:8 NIV). A modern interpretation of this would be to imagine your tears collected by God in a bottle! For those reading this book, know that none of your tears go to waste. God will not allow them to be squandered. He will turn your wailing into dancing and replace your sackcloth with garments of joy (Psalm 31:11).

FEELING ALONE, BUT CALLED

In my life's journey, being singled out didn't mean being alone; in fact, it's quite the opposite. It affirms that we are called for a purpose, a purpose that only we can fulfill. This understanding didn't occur to me in a moment of epiphany; rather, it underscores the significance of growth that unfolded through experiences and the nurturing embrace of a community. The journey isn't about reaching a fixed destination; it's an ongoing process of becoming who you are as a person. I've realized that each movement, step, and hurdle was instrumental in the calling and shaping of the very essence of who I am.

DISCOVERING YOUR PURPOSE

The question of whether we're all singled out can be answered with a resounding "absolutely!" Every individual is chosen for a purpose, a divine calling. The only variable is when this calling is recognized. Some may sense it at a tender age, while others might uncover it later in life. However, it may be an unfortunate reality that some may never understand their purpose, much less fulfill it, but that does not mean they are without purpose. It means they did not understand or refused to acknowledge they had a purpose in the first place. The pivotal factor is the decision to embrace this calling and walk the path as it unfolds.

Here are some recommendations that you may find helpful for discovering your life's purpose:

- *Read inspirational books:* Engaging with inspirational literature can be a transformative experience. These books provide a different perspective, a source of motivation, and a wealth of wisdom. Some of the stories share the joy of overcoming. They offer a chance to learn from the experiences of leaders, thinkers, and change-makers who have made a difference in their lives and the lives of others.

- *Journal:* Journaling is a powerful tool for self-discovery and reflection. It's a private and safe space where you can express your thoughts, frustrations, fears, and aspirations. Then, you can write your hopes and the promises of God and look back to see where things worked out in your favor. Journaling can help you determine your life's purpose.

- *Reflection:* Taking time to reflect on your life is crucial to understanding your purpose. Reflection is more than thinking; it's a process of examining your decisions, past actions, and future goals. This process may reveal patterns in your life and assist with course correction. Reflections help you connect with your inner self and have the internal back-and-forth needed to move forward with your life.

- *Find accountability partners:* Accountability partners can significantly enhance your journey in fulfilling your purpose. These individuals are concerned about your well-being and can share with you the areas where change is needed. This is done in love, not out of malice or self-righteous indignation.

- *Community Service:* Engaging in community service can cause you to focus on someone or something other than yourself. It's an opportunity to give and make a positive impact on the lives of others. It gives a sense of fulfillment, perspective, and enlightenment in serving others.

NAVIGATING HEALTHY AND UNHEALTHY INTERPRETATIONS

The concept of being singled out is open to different interpretations; it can be seen in both positive and negative lights. The healthy interpretation, which I hold dear, is grounded in confidence and faith. This perspective is for those women who recognize their distinctive paths and talents. The journey is not necessarily about external validation but about understanding inner worth and capabilities. There may have been setbacks or discrimination, but they have used those experiences to fuel their determination and resilience, drawing strength from their inner being.

It's about understanding one's uniqueness, recognizing the gifts we possess, and making a profound commitment to serving others. The common thread for this gift is the commitment to serve others, whether through work, advocacy, or community engagement. It is inherently selfless and focused on creating a positive impact on the world.

Unhealthy interpretations have caused many people to navigate the pitfalls of feeling unworthy or unloved. Society often imposes harsh standards and expectations on women, leading to self-doubt and a skewed sense of self-worth. Overcoming these unhealthy interpretations involves a conscious effort to detach self-worth from external validation and societal norms. It's about embracing one's true self, acknowledging both strengths and vulnerabilities, and understanding that worthiness and love are inherent, not conditional.

ADDRESSING THE DARK TIMES

In the midst of difficulty, I found refuge in my faith and gratitude, choosing to let them lead the way. This wasn't about ignoring the hardships I faced; rather, it was a conscious decision to seek out a bright light, even in the darkest of places. It became an intentional practice to cultivate gratitude, shifting my focus from the day-to-day challenges to the abundant blessings showered upon me.

Let me say it again, my life was *difficult!* However, most people have had difficulty at some point and time. I have been through a divorce, I have had difficult jobs, and in a 24-month period, I had 14 late notices on my apartment door. It was *difficult.* I was a single parent going to college full-time, working full-time with mandatory overtime, and had a "side hustle." It was *difficult.* How did I keep up with my bills? I borrowed from my mother and friends. (Just as a side note, I always paid the money I borrowed back, although I borrowed it regularly.) I lost my job; I took care of and eventually lost my Mommy. At the time of writing this book, I lost my Dad. It was *difficult.* Again, but God's grace!

However, in it all and through it all, I had to count my blessings, to truly appreciate the goodness in every moment, no matter how small. My verse I say daily is, "This is the day the Lord has made; I will rejoice and be glad in it" (Psalm 118:24). There was also a song that said, "He is always looking out for me, always busy opening doors that I don't even see, I don't have to worry because He takes good care of me. Oh, it's Jesus looking out for me" (Rev. Jimmie L. Banks). This routine of gratitude became part of my devotion, steering me through the toughest times. It constantly reminds me that even in our darkest hours, it will not always be like this; there is something – One – that propels us towards growth and deeper understanding. My path, peculiar as it may be, echoes the experiences of countless women who have courageously weathered their own storms. It's a narrative of shared resilience, a testament to how we've risen above and continue to stand strong.

This story showcases the immense strength within each of us. By embracing gratitude and faith, we don't merely endure life's challenges; we transform them. They become the very experiences that mold our character, shape our being, and ultimately, lead us to discover our truest, most authentic selves.

A JOURNEY OF UNDERSTANDING

As we explore the concept of being singled out and delve into the myriad interpretations and perspectives, I hope that you'll better understand elements of your own journey. This journey, this exploration into the essence of being "singled out," is about more than just understanding a concept – it's about delving deep into the roots of our personal stories, our struggles, and our triumphs.

Picture yourself embarking on a path of discovery, where your uniqueness isn't just acknowledged but celebrated. It's a journey that calls for not just recognition but also growth, service, and a steadfast commitment to carving out a life that's not just lived, but lived with purpose.

As we walk this path, let's draw strength and inspiration from the heroes of the past, those who were "singled out" for their extraordinary callings. Their stories are not just stories from long ago; they are lessons that are timeless and relevant.

SINGLED OUT HEROES OF PURPOSE

In our journey to understand what it truly means to be "singled out" for a divine purpose, let's draw inspiration from biblical figures who have walked the path before us. These individuals offer invaluable insights into the strength and resilience that come with embracing our unique callings.

- *Shiphrah and Puah - Guardians of Faith*: Leading us to the book of Exodus, Shiphrah and Puah stand firm amidst oppression and cruelty. They respected the Hebrew God, defying the orders of the king of Egypt to protect Hebrew newborns. Their unwavering courage and faith were rewarded with God's kindness, showcasing the power of standing for what is right.

- *Abigail - The Peacemaker*: In 1 Samuel, Abigail, a woman of wisdom and courage, intervened in a tense confrontation between her husband, Nabal, and the future king, David. Her actions prevented potential disaster, highlighting the impact a single individual can have in averting conflict. Abigail teaches us that being singled out can involve the duty to bring peace and harmony to those around us.

- *Tamar - Resilience in the Face of Betrayal*: Genesis introduces Tamar, daughter-in-law to Judah, whose life was marred by betrayal and injustice. Despite her trials, Tamar's bold actions ensured her rights were upheld and Judah's lineage continued. Her story speaks to the resilience required when navigating life's challenges, demonstrating that being singled out for a purpose involves overcoming seemingly insurmountable obstacles.

PERSEVERANCE THROUGH GENERATIONS

We often reflect on the enduring wisdom of historical figures, those luminaries who have guided our paths through their lives and words. Figures like Nelson Mandela, George Washington Carver, and Maya Angelou serve as testaments to change and the power of resilience. Yet, the wisdom that shapes us often comes from sources closer to home, from voices less celebrated but equally profound.

Individuals like Pastor Geneva Crudup, Pastor Paul Brown, Barbara Jones, Betty Jones, Bill Cashaw, Bishop James Nelson, Sr., and Pastor Jason Nelson, just to name a few, have shared their insights and experiences, offering guidance and perspective in moments of doubt and decision. Their words, simple yet profound, have stayed with me, shaping the way I view challenges and opportunities. They have shown me that reaching goals isn't solely about ambition or ability but about wisdom being the principal thing (Proverbs 4:7). Wisdom allows us to recognize our strengths and limitations, to learn from failure, to understand what constitutes "success," and to appreciate that our journey is as important as our destination.

These individuals, along with others, have taught me that the path to our goals is rarely straight; it's a winding road marked by moments of doubt and clarity, setbacks, and triumphs. Along this road, it's the wisdom gleaned from both the extraordinary and the everyday that guides us, helping us navigate life's complexities with grace and determination.

So, as we stand on the shoulders of giants, let's also remember to listen to the quieter voices around us—the ones that offer pearls of wisdom amid our daily lives. Their insights, born out of experience, challenges, and reflection, are the guiding stars that help us chart our course through the ever-changing landscape of life. Their wisdom is a reminder that every one of us has something to contribute, and that each of our stories holds lessons worth sharing. In this sharing, we find not just guidance for ourselves but the chance to inspire and uplift others on their own journeys. This is the elegant collage of human experience, woven together by the threads of wisdom passed down through generations and in the quiet moments of everyday life.

DIVINE PLANS AND GENERATIONAL STRENGTH

Jeremiah 29:11 speaks directly to our hearts, reminding us that the Lord's plans for us are imbued with hope and purpose. It tells us that being "singled out" is not a journey into uncertainty but a path toward a future filled with potential and promise. As we reflect on this, consider the stories of resilience and strength that have personally touched our lives. I often find myself inspired by the enduring spirit of my grandmother, whose life story, set against a backdrop of challenges and adversity, is a powerful example of unwavering strength.

In your own life, you may find similar examples of this generational strength. These stories, whether they come from ancient scriptures or the annals of our family histories, are beacons of strength, purpose, and faith. They remind us that our journeys, though rare, are interconnected by common threads of human experience—the trials, the triumphs, and the unyielding hope that propels us forward. Let us draw strength from the biblical assurances and the personal stories of resilience that surround us. Their combined wisdom serves as a testament to the incredible journeys that lie ahead when we embrace our unique callings with faith and courage.

These stories that I share are not just stories of the past; they are guiding lights for our future. They encourage us to see being singled out not as a burden but as an opportunity to grow, to serve, and to fulfill our God-given potential. In this understanding, we find the strength to face our challenges and the wisdom to appreciate the extraordinary path that each of us walks. Let these scriptures inspire us to live our lives marked by purpose, hope, and a deep commitment to our individual and collective futures.

2

THE SINGLED OUT JOURNEY

In the depths of my life lies a journey – a path filled with emotions, marked by challenges that have tested my spirit, and periods of profound spiritual growth that have shaped who I am to this day. This chapter, this personal narrative, is more than just my story – it's a reflection of a journey that, while unique to me, echoes the experiences and struggles many of us face. This period in my life is a vivid illustration of human resilience, a testament to the strength we all possess, often lying dormant until we face our greatest challenges. It's about those moments of uncertainty and fear, where the only way forward is through sheer grit and determination. It's about the tears shed in private, the doubts that linger in the quiet of the night, and the inner resolve to rise each morning and face the day anew.

But it's not just a story of endurance; it's a narrative deeply interwoven with spirituality. My spiritual journey has been transformative, guiding me through life's obscurities with a sense of purpose and a deeper understanding of the world around me. This spiritual journey has not been about grand revelations; instead, it's been a series of quiet, introspective moments where faith provided solace and strength. It's been about finding meaning in the trials and celebrating the joys, all while staying grounded in a sense of something greater than myself.

This journey of mine is also a celebration of growth and change. Each challenge faced, each obstacle overcome, has been a lesson in itself, teaching me about compassion, empathy, and the unbreakable human spirit. These experiences have not only molded me but have also given me an extraordinary perspective on life, a perspective that I hope resonates with others and offers comfort or inspiration.

So, as I share chapters of my life, remember that each of us is on a journey, filled with our own stories, challenges, and triumphs. Our paths may be distinct, with different twists and turns, but they are all marked by a universal human experience – the pursuit of meaning, the search for inner strength, and the transformative power of spirituality. Let my journey be a reminder that no matter what we face, we possess an incredible capacity for resilience, and with faith and determination, we can navigate the complexities of life with grace and purpose.

EMOTIONS: THE ROLLERCOASTER RIDE OF LIFE

My life resembled a rollercoaster, complete with its own set of exhilarating highs and extremely painful lows. The emotions that came with it were overwhelming, testing the boundaries of my endurance and sanity. The journey began under the shadow of feeling singled out, a sensation tinged with loneliness and a deep sense of being adrift. This unsettling feeling of uncertainty, of feeling isolated and disconnected, is something many of us can relate to. It's that nagging sense of being lost, unsure of one's direction in life, a sentiment that resonates with so many as a common thread in our collective experience. But the essence of this journey isn't found in these feelings alone; it's deeply rooted in the valuable lessons they teach us about ourselves and the world around us.

In my earlier years, I often found myself at the mercy of my emotions. The rollercoaster of peaks and valleys was intense, and I frequently found myself caught in the tumultuous waves of euphoria followed by despair. At that time, mental health wasn't a topic of widespread discussion or understanding. The tools and resources that are more readily available today weren't as accessible, leaving me to navigate these choppy emotional waters largely on my own.

I grappled with these difficulties, facing moments that felt oppressive, even verging on depression. It was a passage through a storm, marked by its fierce winds and unsettling calm. Nevertheless, God places people in your life for your life. There were instances when I was so thankful for two young ladies who actually stayed at my apartment while I battled what was going on in my mind. They literally would stay the night, and one night turned into two nights, etc.

I can remember I was drained, I had a daughter, I was struggling in so many areas of my life, and they were there; they cooked, bought food, and just chit-chatted. They were late teens or early twenties, and they loved being around my daughter. When I would arrive home, they wanted to talk about boys; how ironic, I was going through a divorce, and they wanted to hear about relationships. They were young; I didn't share what was going on in my world, they just wanted to eat bacon and chicken and talk about love and marriage. Little did I know how much these young women "saved" my life. I definitely didn't realize it then.

I can remember one day on a Sunday morning, I could not get out of bed, I was crying and hurting inside. Usually, I would go to church, but didn't stay through the entire service. This day in particular I just felt sick. The two of them noticed that I wasn't in service, and came to my apartment and would not leave my residence until I got dressed and went to church. Was that my deliverance day? It was the demarcation of the turn in another direction. The title of the sermon was "God Remembered Rachel." The preacher said to replace your name with Rachel. I felt better. I felt hope. I felt something break off of me, and all the positive things that were occurring around me, I felt inside of me.

That Sunday, along with many others, taught me invaluable lessons about the power of perseverance, the importance of mental health, and the necessity of seeking support when needed. It showed me that our emotions, no matter how daunting, do not define us. They are but chapters in our larger story, each with its own lessons and insights.

So, as I share additional chapters of my life, I hope it resonates with those who have felt similarly lost or overwhelmed. Remember, you are not alone in these feelings. The journey of navigating through life's highs and lows, of finding your way amidst uncertainty, is a shared human experience. It's a path that, while challenging, can lead to profound growth and a deeper understanding of who we are. Let this story be a reminder of the strength that lies within each of us, the resilience we can muster, and the hope that guides us through even the darkest of times.

THE CHALLENGES FACED

As I mentioned before, the challenges were plenty. From financial difficulties and insurmountable debts to the taxing responsibility of single parenthood, life didn't hand out any free passes.

In addition, the struggle revealed itself through practical challenges, such as difficulties with transportation. I drove my car with holes in the floor and no heat. Survival often meant embracing the simplicity of life, like the famous "cereal ministry" where food options were limited to cereal for breakfast, lunch, and dinner—this was the meal plan in our house. This is also a testament to the strength it takes to endure and the willingness to find hope even when it feels distant.

From the daunting specter of financial challenges and the crushing weight of ridiculous amounts of debt to the singular challenges of single parenthood, life was "life-ing" – it did not offer any shortcuts. Balancing the role of a mother, in itself a monumental task, was made even more complex by parenting the best way I knew how. I vividly recall a conversation with a family member where I expressed that perhaps someone else could offer my child a better upbringing than I could at that particular time. This vulnerability, this fear of not being enough for my child, is a sentiment shared by many parents in similar situations.

In addition, the struggle to further my education was like walking a tightrope. On one hand, there were the long, exhausting hours of work—a necessary endeavor to ensure the safety and stability of our home in a decent community. On the other hand, there was the commitment to college, a pursuit fueled by the hope of a better future for our family. This balancing act, or lack thereof, was nothing short of monumental, a feat that tested the limits of my endurance and resolve.

This chapter of my life is more than just a story of hardships; it's a testament to the resilience required to endure tough times. It's about the strength it takes to keep moving forward, even when the path is obscured by uncertainty. And more importantly, it's about the ability to hold onto hope, to believe in the possibility of a brighter tomorrow even when it feels distant.

So, as I share more experiences, I do so with the understanding that they mirror the struggles of many. It's a reminder that no matter how challenging our circumstances, there's an innate strength within each of us to persevere. And in this perseverance, we find not only the courage to face our trials but also the grace to embrace the lessons they teach us. Let this story be an inspiration to those who find themselves on similar paths, a beacon of hope that illuminates the strength and resilience inherent in all of us.

SPIRITUAL GROWTH: A PATH TO SELF-DISCOVERY

Amidst the chaos, turning points surfaced or little lights of hope would flicker. The journey of spiritual growth became paramount. A sermon that spoke of God's remembrance acted as a demarcation in my life, inspiring faith and anticipation. It opened the doors to an understanding of God as a loving presence, not a punitive figure. The journey was also marked by a chance encounter with a stranger who prophesied, "God has anointed you for such a time as this." These moments ignited a deep, abiding faith and the realization that the

path to spiritual growth started with self-identity, nurturing, and relationships.

There was an instance when I was in my early 30s, my life
looked like strings of spaghetti, all over the place on a plate. I went
home to New Jersey and there, in a supermarket, a lady stopped me
and said, "You are anointed (called out) and God is going to use you
mightily." I thought to myself, this lady has to be kidding; first off, I
am in NJ in a supermarket; secondly, why is she talking to me about
anything at this point, I am trying to shop. But I did not discount
what she said, although I did not feel like anything she said was
accurate. Instead, I journaled the experience. It took time to start to
understand who I 'be' (who I am). I had to recognize my own
temperament, the power of extroversion, and how I influenced relationships—not just with others, but also with God. I started
believing the word and writing words of affirmation. I started
unlocking the door to understanding my unique journey and
mission.

NAVIGATING LIFE'S UNEXPECTED TURNS

In addition to the emotional and spiritual challenges I faced during
the journey within, other significant events occurred in my life, which
further shaped my path.

A new set of challenges emerged. My mother began exhibiting
symptoms of Alzheimer's disease, a condition that would prove to be
both emotionally and mentally taxing for our family. One day, my
mother called me, overwhelmed by her situation. She confessed that
she hadn't paid any of her bills in months and was feeling depressed.
This revelation left me in a state of confusion and uncertainty.

My mother had such strong faith in God. She would often say,
"Saints don't have bad days." Just a side note: I often thought to myself,
I don't know who she is talking about because the struggle was real
over here in my world. I realized later in life that it was not that we
did not have challenges; she just believed that when you have Jesus in
your life, your perspective is different. She believed and trusted God,

also saying she would live to see at least 70 years because that is what is promised to me in His word.

So, to hear my mother say she felt "depressed," I knew there was something wrong and I needed to figure out how to navigate this new chapter in our lives.

In my time of need, a trusted friend offered a piece of invaluable advice to obtain power of attorney, a critical step that allowed me to act legally on my mother's behalf. As a result, I found myself not only caring for my ailing mother, who was diagnosed with Alzheimer's Disease, but also providing for my daughter. This new role as a caregiver placed additional financial strain on our family, intensifying the weight of responsibility that I had to shoulder.

These events added new layers of complexity to my life's journey. As I navigated the challenges within my family, I continued to grapple with my emotions and the pursuit of my spiritual growth. The weight of these responsibilities was considerable, but it became another facet of my story—one that played a crucial role in shaping my resilience and unwavering faith. I prayed and asked God to allow me to be financially stable, knowing that I needed to be able to support my family during this trying time.

Amidst the chaos and uncertainty, moments of clarity emerged. The journey of spiritual growth became paramount, guiding me through the darkest times and offering sparks of optimism. These moments ignited a deep, abiding faith and the realization that the path to spiritual growth started with self-identity, nurturing, and relationships.

I began to embrace the idea that my struggles were not in vain, that there was a purpose behind the challenges I faced. Each obstacle became an opportunity for growth, a chance to deepen my understanding of myself and my relationship with God. I learned to lean on my faith during moments of uncertainty, finding solace in the belief that God had a plan for me, even when I couldn't see it.

Navigating life's unexpected turns became a testament to my resilience and determination. When faced with my mother's illness and the financial strain it brought, I leaned into my faith, trusting that

God would provide a way forward. With the support of trusted friends and the strength of my own convictions, I navigated through the challenges, knowing that I was not alone.

As I reflect on these experiences, I am reminded of the power of faith and resilience. They are the guiding forces that have carried me through the darkest moments of my journey, illuminating the path forward and giving me the strength to persevere. Though the road may be difficult, I know that I am not alone, for God is with me every step of the way. And with His guidance, I am confident that I can overcome any obstacle that comes my way.

LESSONS IN RELATIONSHIPS

This journey had another crucial element: relationships. Understanding my own extroverted nature and how it impacted my interactions with others was instrumental in navigating the perplexities of human connections. I learned that some of my "happiness" was being surrounded by people, but some of those people were unhealthy for me. Early in my life, I did not understand what it meant to have people in my life for a season vs. a lifetime. Many of you may be able to relate; you are hanging onto unhealthy relationships that cause harm, and there is no peace. At some point, you have to "cut the string." Forgive yourself for staying as long as you did in the relationship. It is time to blossom. This knowledge transformed me and helped me when I married my husband. I was able to see my husband for who he truly was as a man of God and not focus on all of the negative experiences in my life as the headlights for our relationship. Was I nervous about getting married? Yes, I was! Did I believe that he was the man for me? After being vetted, yes, I did! Our union also allowed us to guide others in marriage, which has been part of our ministry.

In the end, this journey, replete with emotions, complexity, and spiritual growth, underscores the profound transformation that can occur when faith and service become guiding principles. The lesson is clear: Embrace your uniqueness, your emotions, and your challenges. They are part of your story. As I said earlier, "nothing wasted." Seek a deeper connection with God, find your purpose in serving others, and nurture the relationships that are the cornerstone of your life. Every challenge can be transformed into an opportunity for growth and service. And in this transformation, true purpose is found.

My journey serves as an inspiration—a reminder that we all have the power to embrace our unique path and emerge with a stronger, more profound sense of self, faith, and purpose.

3
NAVIGATING CHALLENGES: A STEP-BY-STEP APPROACH

Every challenge mentioned is to share and show that you are not in this alone. When you find yourself facing circumstances that seem insurmountable, it's natural to feel overwhelmed, defeated, and at your wit's end. However, we're about to explore a few step-by-step approaches that can transform your challenges into stepping stones toward your greater self and help you find hope even in the darkest of hours.

REFOCUSING YOUR THOUGHTS: CHANGING THE NARRATIVE

Often, when life takes a difficult turn, it's hard to believe that it will ever get better. Clichés like "Don't worry" or "Just pray about it" can sound empty in the face of mounting bills, unemployment, or a health crisis. The truth is, it begins with a change in your thought process. Understand that it's a process, and mostly it starts with small steps.

I've encountered countless dilemmas in my life, and it felt like I had hit rock bottom. It's during these moments that I discovered the Lord's love and kindness in unexpected ways. It wasn't necessarily a miraculous rescue from my troubles, but rather a network of friends who constantly checked in on me. They made sure I ate, got out of the house, and even dragged me to church. Day by day, I felt myself moving away from the feeling of drowning and towards the light. The weight I'd carried for so long began to lift, but I couldn't explain it to my friends or family. I didn't even know what was happening; all I knew was that things changed for the better.

CHANGING YOUR SELF-TALK: WHAT YOU BELIEVE, YOU BECOME

Your internal dialogue has immense power. You will believe anything you repeatedly tell yourself. If you're continuously reinforcing negative thoughts, you'll find yourself stuck in a cycle of negativity. Instead, remind yourself of what God says in His Word.

Below are some thoughts and ways to remind you of who you are in Him:

- *Listen to the Preached Word:* There's transformative power in listening to the Word. Allow it to seep into your spirit like a tea bag steeping in water. Feel it, embrace it, and praise God for it. Receive God's word for you in your situation.

- *Self-Reflection*: It's vital to reflect on what you've heard in the past, your dreams, and what's been spoken into your life. However, you should only focus on what's in your best interest—things in line with what God says about you. Think about your passions and your 'why.' Write down things that are lovely, true, and of good report. Concentrate your thoughts on uplifting, life-building ideas.

- *Spiritual Awareness*: Develop an awareness of the ways God speaks to you. Maybe God speaks to you through dreams, an audible voice, Bible study, etc. Look around for His guidance. He may be sharing His wisdom in various, often subtle, ways.

- *Setting Goals*: Consider where you want to be in one, three, and five years. Start small and make progress. You are your own competition. Remember that when you seek the Kingdom of God, everything else falls into place. You are a king or queen in your own kingdom. You have because God's Word says you have. Walk in His Word.

- *Overcoming Fear:* Fear can be paralyzing. I, too, was afraid, fearing the loss of my apartment, my car, opening a business, and writing this book. Fear can be so paralyzing that you become physically ill or have anxiety, but sometimes you must walk through the very fear you feel. Someone said both *fear* and *faith* have voices and we have to argue our case of *faith* like an attorney does, building on it with every word. Talk to yourself, encourage yourself, and keep moving forward, even when fear says you can't.

- *Continuous Learning*: Enrich your knowledge by taking courses or attending workshops on topics that intrigue you. Expand your knowledge, which may lead to discovering a passion that you hadn't previously considered.

- *Patience*: Remember that everything takes time, and sometimes it's not on your schedule but God's divine timing. Realize that the work is done in Heaven. Discovering your purpose may not happen quickly. It's okay not to find answers immediately; the journey itself contributes to personal growth.

- *Taking Action:* The most crucial step is to take action.

Implementing your new mindset and principles into practical steps is key to navigating life's challenges.

Life's struggles will not disappear overnight, but by following these steps and remaining steadfast, you can begin to change your life's trajectory. Remember, the journey is valuable, and it's in these challenges that we often find our deepest purpose.

4

LIVING OUT YOUR PURPOSE

Throughout my personal journey of self-doubt, I've learned that with God, I can triumph over adversity, and that with unwavering belief through faith, every obstacle can be conquered. The narrative of my life has been one filled with twists and turns, from the early seeds of doubt to discovering the inner strength that allows me to not just survive, but thrive.

CHASING OPPORTUNITIES AND DISCOVERING FAITH

Regarding my job situation, I was finally promoted to a managerial position. However, the lack of financial security led me to seek other opportunities with other companies. I was recruited by a large corporation, but my decision to leave my current employer took an unexpected twist. The Program Manager informed me that opportunities were on the horizon within our division. He emphasized that my performance was exceptional, leading me to believe that I would be considered for one of the new opportunities in the company. Excited by the news he shared, I decided to rescind my job offer. Approximately four weeks later, I had a vivid dream that would become an unsettling reality.

My girlfriends would often share their dreams with me, and I'd dismiss them as mere coincidences. However, this dream, my dream, felt very real as if I was in the room before the inevitable happened; this dream soon manifested into a harrowing premonition of my future.

The dream displayed my name written on a piece of paper that was placed on a long conference table—a seemingly innocuous dream that evolved into a disturbing reality that would test my faith.

The next day at work, an unusual atmosphere filled the office as high-ranking executives from New Jersey, including the Vice President and Division Managers, showed up—an unprecedented occurrence. The Manager who had assured me of new opportunities announced his transfer to another organization. I assumed that his career was taking a favorable turn, but what transpired next produced a shockwave that rippled through the office.

One after another, Senior Managers began calling employees into a conference room and delivered the grim news: they were being laid off. For someone who had never experienced such a situation, I was thrust into an unsettling new reality. Nervously, I called my mother and a friend of mine, urging them to pray for me. The dream manifested itself—my name was on the list.

Bracing myself for the meeting, I entered the room. There, I saw my manager who seemed defeated, his eyes red from the emotion of hearing his subordinates scream and cry as they were told they would no longer be employed at a company that many had worked for over 10, 15, and 20 years. Across from me sat a Division Manager from New Jersey, her expression void of sentiment.

The meeting unfolded, discussing the next steps for my current department, and culminated in my pending layoff as of a date she shared with me. I was given a "package." I did not cry, scream, or even sigh heavily. I did not respond to any of the offers that were suggested or recommended to me. I said I would need to review the information and walked away with decorum and did not allow the energy or the environment to cloud my judgment of seeking necessary guidance for the next steps until I went home and cried.

I had lost 25 pounds from the emotional toll that weighed heavily on my heart and the questions that were racing in my mind. How would I take care of my child? It was during this time that I prayed to God and asked Him to give me the resources that I needed to take care of my family. I felt isolated. I did not have a plan or a solution. But I believed that God answers prayers. God had done it before. Sometimes you have to focus on what you are able to do vs. being persuaded by the things you have no control over in your life. I did not tell them to fire me. I didn't want to be in this situation. I can remember someone asked me how I was doing. I said, "I am doing GREAT!" She said, "You found a job?" I said, "No, but this will be my answer when I do." During this time, I had to walk by faith and rely on God as my Father.

MAINTAIN YOUR RELATIONSHIP WITH GOD

I've learned the necessity of maintaining a strong connection with God, keeping faith at its core. It's vital to reflect on this, especially when trying to break free from life's repetitive downward cycles. Grounded in faith, you can escape these never-ending loops where you find yourself repeating the same mistakes and experiencing the same hardships year after year.

I've pondered this a lot, and it struck me that staying grounded in faith is the key to breaking free from this cycle. Recently, I've heard from someone who has a profound affinity for the Book of Genesis. Essentially, there are three simple steps to fullness: "Be, Do, Have" (Myron Golden). This concept resonated deeply with me, and I'd like to share it with you.

First, we start with "be." It's about understanding and embracing who you truly are. The Bible tells us that we are the head and not the tail, above only and not beneath. Recognizing this is where it all begins; it's acknowledging that you are a child of God, uniquely designed for greatness.

Once you truly understand who you are, the next step is "do." You begin to take action according to your divine calling. Every one of us possesses unique gifts and talents, bestowed upon us by God. Some sing, some cook, some write, mentor, or own businesses. It's your mission to discover your unique gift and put it to use.

There's a profound concept in scripture about time and chance. It's not just about seizing opportunities when they arise. It signifies that when time and opportunity intersect, extraordinary things happen. This is the "have." This intersection will occur in each of our lives, and the crucial aspect is to be prepared when that opportunity arrives.

In times of encounters and isolation, remember that this, too, is part of your purpose. Even when you feel alone or isolated, understand that you are singled out for a special purpose. Don't compare your journey to others. Everyone's path is distinct. Your unique set of challenges and opportunities sets you on your own course.

Maintaining a strong relationship with God is the anchor you need during these times. Think of it as your navigational system. God is with you throughout your journey, providing guidance even when you encounter unexpected obstacles. You might find yourself in dark woods, facing seemingly endless nights, but remember that God is your navigator, leading you to your destination.

When you are isolated for a purpose, remember that it doesn't mean you're alone without a purpose. Being a single parent is a prime example. It doesn't make you any less capable or valuable. You are isolated for a reason. God has a plan for you, and He has equipped you with unique gifts and strengths.

Let me address single mothers. You, like many others, face unique challenges. Feeling alone in this situation is a common experience, but it's essential to remember that you still have a purpose. Regardless of your family structure, your vision, and your giftings, you are still a benefactor of God's grace. What matters most is not what you lack but what you do with what you have. Everything you need is already in you.

God has the ability to multiply even the smallest things we offer, much like the widow and her son in the Bible (1 Kings). She thought that she would make her last meal for her son and die. However, what she didn't know was that God was going to show her the power of using what she had and multiply it. Therefore, don't ever underestimate your gift with God. It's not about addition; it's about multiplication. God will use what you have and multiply it to make a lasting impact.

Each of us charts a distinct path through life. You can't compare your path to someone else's because you don't know the challenges, tests, and their experiences in their life. Focus on being the best version of yourself today and strive to improve day by day. It's not about following someone else's story; it's about creating your own. When God isolates you for a purpose, you can trust that He will never leave you stranded. He's guiding you to your destination, even when the path seems unclear.

Maintain a strong relationship with God and stay grounded in faith. This journey involves self-discovery, understanding who you are in Christ, and aligning your actions with your God-given purpose. Your faith in God serves as the foundation for growth, and that faith helps you continue to progress, even in the face of challenges.

One of the most essential elements in nurturing your relationship with God is dedicating time with Him. It's about developing an intimate connection through prayer and reflecting on His Word. Like in any relationship, you need one-on-one time to get to know someone better. As you grow in your understanding of God's love for you, you will start to reflect His character.

However, there's another significant factor often overlooked in one's journey. As people of color, we sometimes allow external influences and distractions to shape our self-perception. Single mothers may lack positive role models, leading us to form distorted self-images. Instead, we should recognize the gifts God has blessed us with and focus on them. By shifting our attention from distractions like television, social media, excessive phone use, or unfruitful conversations and instead concentrating on understanding our purpose and calling, we can change not only ourselves but people connected to us.

We must also be cautious of time-wasters. People often claim they don't have enough time. The truth is, we all have time; it's about refocusing on what truly matters. As mentioned earlier, it's all about multiplication versus addition. God multiplies our efforts, and it's up to us to use our time and gifts wisely.

5

ADDRESSING COMMON CRITICISMS

In this chapter, we will delve into common criticisms and misconceptions that often surround the concept of being singled out. These criticisms can come from both external and internal sources, creating hurdles that we must overcome to pursue our aspirations.

As we walk this route of discovering what it means to be singled out, we must be prepared to respond to skepticism and criticism. These critical voices, whether they come from others or from the nagging doubts within, can be frustrating.

Let's begin by addressing some of the most common criticisms and misconceptions you might encounter:

- *Criticism #1: "Who do you think you are, and why do you believe you're good enough to do anything?"*

This question attempts to undermine your confidence. Therefore, a wise response could be, "I am a creation of God, designed with unique purpose and potential. I don't have to prove my worth; it's inherently granted by the One who crafted me. My journey is about discovering and living up to that potential, rather than seeking validation from external voices."

- *Criticism #2: "You're going to fall on your face."*

This is a fear that many of us face – the fear of failure. But remember, failures are not terminal; they're stepping stones to success (nothing wasted). Embrace them and learn from your mistakes. Therefore, your response could be, "Falling is just part of the learning process. Each setback brings me a step closer to my goals. My failures do not define me, but my resilience and determination do."

- *Criticism #3: "What makes you feel qualified for your dreams?"*

This question often circles back to imposter syndrome, where you may doubt your own capabilities. A wise response would be, "I don't need external validation to follow my dreams. I'm not defined by my qualifications; I'm driven by my passion and purpose. My commitment to learning and growing is what qualifies me."

- *Criticism #4: "You have to be a certain way, look a certain way, speak a certain way, or fit a stereotype."*

This criticism is born from societal expectations. The truth is, "I refuse to be limited by societal norms or stereotypes. I am my authentic self, and that's where my strength lies. Singling out doesn't mean fitting in; it means standing out as my true self."

- *Criticism #5: "You'll never get past this point."*

We all face moments when it seems impossible to move forward. As I write this book, I felt as if the book would not be published. Again, life was "life-ing." But I had to remind myself while I was sharing with others about the truth of God, "I've faced seemingly insurmountable challenges before. I thought my grief would never end, my divorce would consume me, or my educational dreams would remain unattained. Yet, I persevered. There's always a path forward, even when it's hidden momentarily."

In the face of criticism and misconceptions, it's essential to hold onto a few key solutions. We must be equipped to find the lie within these doubts and address it head-on. Our journey to be singled out requires us to understand that our worth isn't contingent on external factors but on our unique design and divine purpose. We don't merely receive what we see around us or listen to others' viewpoints; instead, we engage in the truth of what God reveals to us in His Word.

Recognize that God has already played His part in our journey; He has laid the foundation for our purpose. However, we must actively receive what's already been done and trust the process. It's a beautiful act of faith, much like singing songs of affirmation over ourselves, journaling our reflections and progress, and, above all, believing in the Word of Truth.

To dispel fear and anxiety along the way, remember this: After you've been delivered from these negative emotions or situations, be vigilant and guard against the resurgence of negative thoughts attempting to reassert their hold on your life. The moment you sense them, don't give up. These emotions are reminders of the battles you've already won, battles that only made you stronger. If you find that you've taken a detour or stumbled, don't be discouraged. Just go back on your path with determination and a reinforced sense of purpose.

Our journey towards being singled out is one of self-discovery, resilience, and faith in the power that guides us. Let's press on and move forward with conviction, for our steps are ordered by God, and there's no challenge too great to overcome.

6

EMBRACING HOPE AND PURPOSE

Life can often throw us into a whirlwind of confusion, doubt, and frustration, leaving us struggling to find our sense of purpose. In such moments, remember that hope is never truly lost, and your purpose is waiting to be discovered.

EMBRACE THE PROCESS

Ecclesiastes 9:10 imparts profound wisdom that we should carry in our hearts during moments of uncertainty. It reminds us that whatever we find to do with our hands, we should do it with all our might. Life's journey is a process, and it's crucial to embrace it with determination and wholehearted effort. Purpose isn't always found at the end of the road; it's often revealed during the journey itself. Every step you take, every challenge you face, and every experience you encounter is a piece of the puzzle that makes up your unique purpose. Embrace the process, even when it seems arduous or unclear, and trust that every moment is significant.

LISTEN TO THE VOICE WITHIN

God communicates with us through thoughts, ideas, and gentle nudges within our hearts. Sometimes, these are soft whispers amidst the chaos of life. To discover your purpose, you must learn to listen to the Voice that speaks within you. Pay attention to those persistent thoughts, recurring ideas, and the inner nudges that tug at your soul. It is in these moments of inspiration that you may find the path to your purpose. Keep a journal, meditate, or simply create quiet moments in your life to tune in to this inner Voice. Often, purpose begins as a subtle murmur, and it's our duty to listen carefully.

TRANSFORM AND RENEW YOUR MIND

Discovering your unique purpose often requires a transformation of your mind. This transformation entails renewing your thoughts and shedding old beliefs that may have held you back. Remember, God's plans for you are unique, and they might not always align with societal norms or expectations. To grow on your journey to purpose, you must be willing to transform your thinking. Release self-doubt, let go of fear, and embrace the new possibilities that God is guiding you towards. In Romans 12:2, the Bible encourages us not to conform to the patterns of this world but to be transformed by the renewing of our minds.

Consider these practical steps to renew your mind:

- *Meditation and Prayer:* Regular meditation and prayer can help calm your mind and create a space for God to speak to you.

- *Reading and Learning:* Expand your knowledge and understanding of the world, both spiritually and intellectually. Reading inspirational books, studying scripture, and learning new things can open your mind to fresh ideas and insights.

- *Seek Guidance:* Connect with wise mentors, counselors, or spiritual leaders who can offer guidance and support along your journey.

- *Positive Affirmations:* Replace negative self-talk with positive affirmations. Remind yourself daily of your worth, purpose, and potential.

- *Step Out of Your Comfort Zone:* Growth often occurs outside your comfort zone. Challenge yourself to step into new experiences and expand your horizons.

- *Practicing Gratitude:* Cultivate gratitude by acknowledging the blessings in your life. A grateful heart is more open to receiving inspiration and recognizing purpose.

PRACTICAL STEPS FOR TRANSFORMATION

As you embrace your unique process, you may encounter moments where you feel stuck. Feeling stuck is a common experience for many, but the journey to embracing your unique purpose is never out of reach.

Let's explore some practical steps to help you move forward:

1. *Seek Inspiration:* Read books or listen to podcasts about personal growth, purpose, and fulfillment. Seek inspiration from others who have walked a similar path. Their stories can be a beacon of hope during challenging times.

2. *Values Assessment:* Consider which values are most important to you. Whether it's integrity, community, creativity, or

another value, understanding this can guide you toward a purpose in alignment with your beliefs. It's crucial because if you're unclear about your values, you may end up following the crowd when making decisions.

3. *New Experiences:* Pursue new experiences—volunteer opportunities, travel, or any activity you haven't tried before. Sometimes, it's in the new and unfamiliar that we discover our true passions.

4. *Feedback from Others:* Occasionally, ask your closest friends, those who have your best interests at heart, about your strengths and weaknesses. They can provide valuable insights into your talents and abilities that you might not see in yourself.

5. *Professional Guidance:* Consider consulting a therapist or counselor who can offer tools and strategies to help you discover your purpose. Sometimes, having professional guidance can provide the clarity needed to take the next step.

6. *Community Involvement:* Engage in the community. Being part of a collective can often help you find purpose through connection and service. Participate in volunteer work or join groups that share your values.

PERSONAL INSIGHTS

This book has been inside of me for over a decade, and it is a light. I am not a "writer," but I see God as a guiding force in my life. He is not a genie in a bottle, but He is undoubtedly a *good, good* Father. When we ask for something according to His purpose, He hears us, and in gratitude, we say thank you with the utmost sincerity. As I stated, I am not a "writer," but I am an Author. It is by God's grace.

In moments of doubt or despair, remember that every step you take is part of your purposeful journey. Whether you're certain about your path or still searching, the process itself is a significant part of your unique purpose. Embrace the hope and encouragement that you are exactly where you are meant to be, and your purpose will be revealed in its own perfect time. God must be the center of your life, your joy, your everything.

In the end, as we navigate life's labyrinth, we must trust that not only will we discover our purpose, but we'll also create a life in which we are at peace with ourselves and the world. In this way, we become a beacon of hope and inspiration to others, who, too, may be searching for their distinct path.

GOD IS ALWAYS LOOKING OUT FOR YOU AND ME

There are moments in life that resonate deeply, reminding us of God's constant presence and His unwavering protection. These are the moments that fill us with awe and gratitude. For example, when my daughter's appendix burst, she mustered the strength to drive herself to the hospital. The doctor's words upon arrival were nothing short of miraculous: "You came in just in time." It was a vivid illustration of divine timing and protection.

Then there were the car accidents, accidents that, by all accounts, should have resulted in severe injuries or worse. Yet, by the grace of God, we walked away from these accidents without needing hospitalization. These are the inexplicable moments where God's protective hand is undeniable.

During late-night walks, which are often considered perilous, I would walk alone after weekend college or from other places, yet I remained unscathed and unharmed, thanks to God's protection. These are moments that reveal God's watchful care. There were fires, threats on my life, and countless other miracles where God's protection and victory were evident. These experiences serve as tangible reminders of His presence in my life.

DAILY BLESSINGS

Every day, as we wake up, we are loaded with blessings that sometimes go unnoticed. We can hear, but we often forget to truly listen.
We have eyes, yet fail to see the wonder of every day. Our bodies
function seamlessly, with countless intricate processes we don't fully
comprehend, but for which we should be grateful.

The truth is that God loads us daily with benefits, both big and
small. It's essential to cultivate a sense of awareness, to truly listen and
observe, and to recognize these daily blessings. It's a testament to
God's boundless love and care, and these everyday miracles are the
subtle whispers of His presence in our lives.

* * *

Your journey to discover your unique purpose is a path filled with
obstacles, yet adorned with moments of divine protection, inspiration, and transformation.

Embrace the process, listen to God's guiding voice, renew your
mind, and recognize His protective hand in your life. You have gained
the strength to move forward with unshakable faith and confidence.
Though your purpose may sometimes seem elusive, it patiently awaits
your discovery, and God faithfully leads you along this journey.

Maintain your trust in Him and stand steadfast, unmovable,
knowing that He is always watchful. Fulfilling your purpose is a work
in progress, and God is the loving artist shaping your life. Remember
to be grateful for His daily blessings, as He continually fills your life
with love and benefits.

7

YOUR NEXT STEPS: EMBRACING YOUR UNIQUE PURPOSE

At this point, it's essential to recap the transformative journey we've undertaken together. Our voyage has encompassed a profound exploration of faith, self-discovery, and the realization of purpose.

Let's now delve into the key points and insights you've encountered:

1. *Isolate for a Purpose:* At times, life may instill a sense of solitude, akin to the feelings experienced by single mothers. Yet, remember, isolation doesn't equate to purposelessness. You are crafted with intent; your strength, purpose, and vision are unique to you. Despite your circumstances, your gifts and God's grace remain accessible. Rather than comparing your path to others', embrace the distinctiveness of your journey and trust in God's plan for you.

2. *Be Authentic:* The central message resonates throughout: "Be authentic." This principle is rooted in faith, and the cornerstone of a strong bond with God lies in comprehending our identity in Him. Scripture reminds us that we are the head and not the

tail, above and not beneath. By uncovering and embracing our true selves, we unlock the gateway to our God-given purpose.

3. *Fulfill Your Calling:* Once we grasp our identity, the subsequent step is to act upon it. God has bestowed each of us with unique gifts and talents. It's our responsibility to employ these gifts to fulfill our divine calling. When we discern our calling and align our actions with it, we unleash our full potential.

4. *Embrace Abundance:* As we tread our purposeful path, we gradually transition to the third phase: "having." Just as the Book of Genesis elucidates, experiencing an abundant life stems from being true to ourselves and fulfilling our intended purpose. Along this journey, we come to grasp God's promises: joy, peace, fulfillment, and a life brimming with His blessings.

5. *Embrace The Power of Multiplication:* Similar to the narratives of the widow and the loaves and fishes in the Bible, God can multiply even the smallest offerings we present. What counts isn't the magnitude of your scarcity but rather how you utilize what you possess. Employ your unique gifts and talents to make a significant impact in the world.

FINAL WORDS OF ENCOURAGEMENT

Embracing your unique self can be an invigorating and life-changing journey. As you walk this path, remember that your life is a testament to God's promises. You are not alone; He is with you every step of the way.

Trust that your isolation, your unique challenges, and your special gifts are all part of God's grand design. Your journey is unlike anyone else's. Embrace it, celebrate it, and use it to fulfill the unique purpose God has crafted for you.

MY PRAYER FOR YOU

May you be who you are, do what you're called to do, and have the abundant life that God has prepared for you. May you find purpose in your isolation, strength in your uniqueness, and fulfillment in the art of multiplication.

Keep the faith, stay grounded, and remember that God is by your side, guiding you through every challenge and opportunity. Embrace your original purpose, for it is your divine calling and God's promise of an abundant life.

* * *

Thank you for joining me on this journey, and I pray that your path is filled with joy, fulfillment, and blessings beyond measure.

ACKNOWLEDGMENTS

The accomplishment of this book is a significant milestone that would not have been possible without the support, love, and encouragement of so many impactful individuals. As I reflect on this journey, my heart overflows with gratitude for the people who have walked beside me, inspired me, and uplifted me along the way. But more importantly, I am forever grateful to God. Without Him, I am absolutely nothing.

- *To my beloved mother,* who transitioned in April 2016, and my cherished father, who transitioned during the writing of this book in February 2024 – your unwavering love and the introduction to Christ at such an early age have been the cornerstones of my life. I am forever grateful.

- *To my wonderful husband,* whose love, encouragement, and unwavering support have been my constant source of strength.

- *To my daughter, daughter-in-love, and bonus sons* – you all have been singled out by God, and I cherish each of you dearly.

- *To my sister, Tara; my brother, Talmon; my sister/cousins, Tori, Trecia, Tracy, and Tia (TJs);* and *my nieces and nephew, Chantrel, Trenee, ByShawn, Tayla, and Terrence,* respectively – thank you for always being there.

- *To the Burnett/Cromartie Family* – thank you for accepting us.

- *To my Sister/Girlfriends, The Nelsons, Natalie, and my other nieces/nephew (JN and SW)* – your friendship means the world to me.

- *Peggy Jones* – you have been a listening ear since I can remember.

- *To my Pastors Jason and Tonya Nelson, and my Tab Church family* – thank you for your spiritual guidance and support.

- *To Nicole Queen and Vision Publishing House* – thank you for the gentle push to finish this book. You are amazing.

Thank you all for your unwavering support, love, and encouragement throughout this journey. Each of you has played an integral role in bringing this vision to life, and I am profoundly thankful for your contributions. Your presence in my life has been a blessing, and I am deeply grateful.

ABOUT THE AUTHOR

Tiana Burnett is a dedicated business owner and real estate investor. She serves on the Board at her local assembly and offers pre-marital support to couples along the East Coast.

Tiana is also the Director of the non-profit BGKingdom Hope Foundation, which empowers children in underprivileged areas by teaching them essential leadership skills.

She currently resides in Maryland, and is happily married with three children.

* * *

To get in touch with Tiana Burnett, please contact her here:
Email: admin@bgkingdom.com

www.ingramcontent.com/pod-product-compliance
Lightning Source LLC
Chambersburg PA
CBHW051554120626
46551CB00013B/1512

* 9 7 8 1 9 5 5 2 9 7 6 3 9 *